FROM AN IDEA TO

LEGO

# FROM AN IDEA TO

# LEGO

## The Building Bricks Behind the World's Largest Toy Company

## LOWEY BUNDY SICHOL

illustrated by C. S. JENNINGS

HOUGHTON MIFFLIN HARCOURT
Boston   New York

hmhbooks.com

The text was set in ITC Galliard Std.

Library of Congress Cataloging-in-Publication Data
Names: Sichol, Lowey Bundy, author.
Title: From an idea to Lego : the building bricks behind the world's
largest toy company / by Lowey Bundy Sichol.
Description: Boston : Houghton Mifflin Harcourt, [2019] | Series:
From an idea to . . . ; 3
Identifiers: LCCN 2018016631| ISBN 9781328954930
(paper over board) | ISBN 9781328954947 (pbk.)
Subjects: LCSH: LEGO koncernen (Denmark)—Juvenile literature. |
LEGO toys—History—Juvenile literature. | Toy industry—Denmark—
History—Juvenile literature.
Classification: LCC HD9993.T694 L4475 2019 | DDC
338.7/688725--dc23
LC record available at https://lccn.loc.gov/2018016631

Printed in the United States of America
DOC 10 9 8 7 6 5 4 3 2 1
4500759255

*For Beekey & Grampy—LEGO is the story of "learning through play" meets business smarts. I can't think of two better people to dedicate this book to. Thank you for everything.*

# Table of Contents

"Only the best is good enough."
—Ole Kirk Christiansen,
founder of LEGO

## Have you ever wondered what the *business story* behind LEGO is?

It may seem like LEGO has been around forever. The reality is that LEGO has been around for more than three generations. That means you, your parents, and even your grandparents may have all built fantastic creations with LEGO.

Today, all things LEGO are produced by a company called the LEGO Group, and hundreds of millions of children *and* adults play with billions of LEGO pieces every day. But almost one hundred years ago, LEGO was just an idea. An idea that a carpenter had to earn money while raising his four young boys. He began by making wooden toys and eventually launched a building system that changed the toy industry forever.

This is the story of LEGO and how little plastic bricks, like the ones scattered across your bedroom floor, helped create the biggest toy company in the world.

# 1 Ole Kirk Christiansen

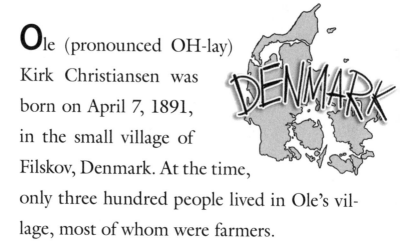

Ole (pronounced OH-lay) Kirk Christiansen was born on April 7, 1891, in the small village of Filskov, Denmark. At the time, only three hundred people lived in Ole's village, most of whom were farmers.

"Life is a gift, but it's more than just that. Life is a challenge."
—Ole Kirk Christiansen

Life was hard for the Christiansen family. His parents, Jens Niels and Kirstine Christiansen, had ten children to care for, and Ole was the youngest. They had only enough money to provide the necessities—food, clothing, shelter, and schooling.

At the young age of seven, Ole went to work on a nearby farm to help earn money for his family. When he wasn't working or attending school, Ole enjoyed making things out of

wood, and over time, he became quite good at it.

When Ole was fourteen, he worked for his older brother, Kristian, as an apprentice carpenter. Ole trained for six years, from 1905 to 1911. After his apprenticeship was over, he spent the next five years serving in the military, studying at the Haslev Technical School, and working as a carpenter in both Germany and Norway.

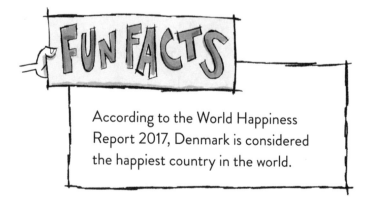

# FUN FACTS

According to the World Happiness Report 2017, Denmark is considered the happiest country in the world.

During that time, Ole also met a woman named Kirstine and they fell in love.

In 1916, Ole and Kirstine returned home to Denmark and were married. They moved to a small town called Billund, which had only a handful of farms, a grocery store, a dairy, a blacksmith, one inn, and a school. There, he bought the Billund Carpentry Shop and Lumberyard for ten thousand Danish kroner (or approximately sixteen hundred dollars).

Ole was a very skilled carpenter, and took great pride in the craftsmanship of his work.

He hired a handful of carpenters, and together they built doors, cabinets, and cupboards, as well as entire houses, stables, dairies, and churches for the local townspeople.

The Billund Carpentry Shop and Lumberyard had a house attached to the back, where Ole and Kirstine lived. They had four sons—Johannes (born in 1917), Karl (born in 1919), Godtfred (born in 1920), and Gerhardt (born in 1926).

Ole was a wonderful father and loved children. He was involved in his church and its

Sunday school. He helped with the church's scouting program for boys and girls. And he taught children at the local Handicrafts School. When Ole needed inspiration or quiet, he spent time gardening and beekeeping.

## THE FIRST FIRE

One Sunday afternoon in 1924, five-year-old Karl and four-year-old Godtfred were playing in Ole's workshop. While trying to light a hot

glue machine, the young boys accidentally set fire to some wood shavings. The fire grew from a small flame to a raging blaze that engulfed the entire factory and house, burning them to ashes.

Despite the property loss, Ole was relieved that no one was injured. He remained calm, kept a positive outlook, and took this opportunity to rebuild his workshop. Ole hired an architect named Jesper Jespesen, who designed a new factory that was even larger and grander than the first.

# HARD TIMES

The year 1930 marked the start of a difficult time for Ole. By then, the **Great Depression**

> **Great Depression:** A period of time (1929–39) when the world's economy collapsed. Millions of people lost their jobs, and many lost their homes, possessions, and all of their money. People struggled to afford necessities such as food, clothes, and shelter. Many stood in line for hours just for a free loaf of bread.

had reached Denmark and deeply affected Ole's carpentry business. Farmers and villagers could no longer afford his products and services. Ole resorted to making less expensive items

> **Layoff:** The loss of a job for business reasons, such as when a company cuts costs, has a work shortage, or is downsizing. Layoffs can affect a group of any size.

such as ladders, stools, and ironing boards. But even with these new pieces, he did not earn enough money to be able to pay his employees their salaries, and he was forced to have **layoffs**.

> The *krone* (plural *kroner*) is the official currency of Denmark, Greenland, and the Faroe Islands.

Then, just two years later, tragedy struck. In 1932, Kirstine died suddenly. Ole was not only devastated by the unexpected passing of his loving wife, but was also concerned about raising his four boys, ages six to fifteen, all by himself.

# 2 Construction Begins

Times were very hard for Ole, and he became worried. The Billund Carpentry Shop was not making any money. Ole couldn't support his own family or buy enough food to feed his sons. He needed to think of something else to help earn money.

One day, Ole used a handful of wood

"Not until the day when I said to myself, 'You must choose between carpentry and the toys' did things start to make sense."
—Ole Kirk Christiansen

scraps from his factory to create some toys for his children. They were thrilled to play with such well-built, high-quality toys. Ole thought that if playing with wooden toys made his own boys happy and helped them forget some of the hard times from the Depression, it was sure to make other children happy too. And he was right!

Ole began making many different types of toys from wood, including racecars, fire trucks, animals, and blocks. He was resourceful and used unsold wooden yo-yos as wheels for

brand-new trucks and pull-along toys. To help his father, Godtfred—who was twelve at the time—became Ole's assistant in the workshop. Godtfred helped sand, paint, and package the toys, as well as keep track of sales.

Word spread about the high-quality hand-crafted toys made and sold in Ole's small workshop in Billund, and sales began to grow. His bestseller became a pull-along wooden duck that opened and closed its beak as it moved. When Ole had too many toys in stock, he loaded them in his car and traveled around the country, selling them door to door. Often, people could only afford to exchange food for the toys, but that was okay. Ole always accepted a good deal and was grateful to be able to provide enough food for his four growing boys.

## SNAPPING TOGETHER A NAME

By 1934, Ole had sold enough toys that he decided he needed a good name for his toy

company, a **brand name**. He wanted it to be short and stand for all the things his toys were—fun, high quality, and all about play. In Danish, the language Ole spoke, the term *leg godt* means "play well." After some time thinking about it, he combined *leg* and *godt* to create a new word—LEGO!

# BUSINESS BASICS— BUILDING A BRAND

## WHAT'S A BRAND NAME?

A brand name is a name chosen to represent a company or product. Brand names should capture what the company or product is about and be chosen carefully, because once established, they are hard to change. They should have a clear meaning, be connected to the company or product in some way, and be easy to pronouce. Brand names are often chosen from one of seven categories:

**DESCRIPTIVE**—describing what the company does (e.g., American Airlines, Whole Foods, Kentucky Fried Chicken)

**SUGGESTIVE**—suggesting an experience or image (e.g., Pampers, Swiffer, Joy)

**COMPOUND**—combining two or more words (e.g., YouTube, PayPal, SpotHero)

**CLASSICAL**—based on Greek or Roman imagery (e.g., Nike, Pandora)

**ARBITRARY**—a real word with no relationship to the company (e.g., Apple, Twitter, Shell)

**MADE UP**—imaginary words (e.g., Dasani, Kleenex)

**NAME**—the founder's name (e.g., Adidas, Ford, Disney)

It's always good to check what the brand name means in other languages. There are many examples where a word has a much different meaning! For example, Hulu, the on-demand TV company, means "cease and desist" in Swahili. There's a detergent in Iran called Barf, which means "snow" in Persian, the Iranian language. There's even a candy bar in Poland called Fart Bar, which means "lucky bar" in Polish, but Fart Bar isn't so lucky in English!

 Sales continued to grow as Ole expanded with more types of toys, such as wooden animals, sailboats, tractors, and board games. He hired seven employees, who were carpenters like him, to help with the increased workload. Day after day, Ole insisted that every single detail mattered; LEGO produced only the highest-quality toys. His rules were clear—each toy was hand-cut from the finest birch wood, carefully sanded, primed, painted, and finished with three coats of lacquer, then beautifully packaged before being shipped out by train.

# FUN FACTS

In Latin, the word *lego* means "I put together." Ole did not know this when he chose the name for his company.

# LESSON LEARNED

One day, young Godtfred announced to his father that he had saved LEGO a lot of money. Proudly looking down on his son, Ole asked him how. Godtfred explained that he had prepared and packed up several boxes of toys with only *two* coats of lacquer on them instead of three. But instead of being pleased, Ole was furious! He instructed Godtfred to return to the train station and retrieve all the boxes of toys with only two coats of lacquer. Then Ole made Godtfred work all night long, carefully brushing a third and final coat of lacquer on each and every toy before he was allowed to go to bed.

Ole's personal motto was

21

*Det bedste er ikke for godt,* which means "Only the best is good enough." This motto was Ole's way of enforcing high **quality control**. After this incident, Godtfred wrote his father's motto on a wooden sign and hung it in the workshop so every employee would be inspired and never try to take a shortcut again.

**Quality control:** The process by which a company reviews the manufacturing of its products and ensures acceptable quality. Some companies, like LEGO, have a very high level of quality control and any bricks with defects are discarded. Other companies are a bit more relaxed. For example, have you ever had two or three crackers stuck together in a box? Those crackers slipped through quality control.

# 3 Brick by Brick

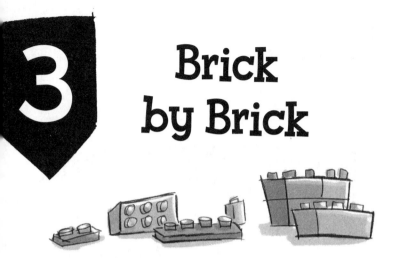

**T**ime passed and Godtfred continued to help Ole run LEGO. In 1939, Europe entered World War II, but despite the hard times, sales at LEGO grew. Parents continued to buy LEGO's wooden toys because they were a small thing that brought joy to their children. This was good news for LEGO.

"I look to the future with hope."
—Ole Kirk Christiansen

In fact, during the first two years of the war, sales doubled.

## A SECOND FIRE

Then calamity struck again in 1942. On a cold and blustery evening in March, a short circuit in the wood factory's electrical wires sparked another fire. Before the fire trucks could arrive, the entire building burned to the ground.

> **Inventory:** The entire stock of a business, including materials, components, work in progress, and finished products.

Though the adjoining house was saved, everything in the factory was destroyed, including LEGO's **inventory** and Ole and Godtfred's drawings and models for all the toys.

## REBUILDING AGAIN

Ole was devastated and considered giving up altogether. But then he thought about his family and his forty employees and how they were all counting on him. It was enough inspiration to change his mind. Ole picked himself up and

persevered. He had a third factory constructed that was, again, bigger and grander than the one before.

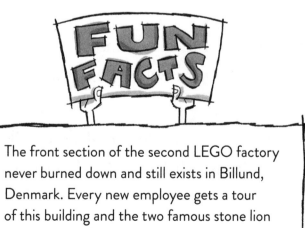

The front section of the second LEGO factory never burned down and still exists in Billund, Denmark. Every new employee gets a tour of this building and the two famous stone lion statues that stand guard at the front door.

# A PLASTIC IMPRESSION

World War II ended in 1945 and Ole and Godtfred were determined to find new ways to expand their toy business. They listened to **customer feedback** from LEGO's primary

**Customer feedback:** The process of gathering customers' opinions about a business, product, or service. Customer feedback is important because it provides insight into how a company can improve its products.

customers—mothers. Moms complained that LEGO's wooden toys were hard to clean and absorbed dirt and germs. Since many great ideas stem from *solving a problem,* Ole was driven to solve this one. He wanted to find a way to build toys that were made out of something more hygienic than wood.

One day, in 1946, Ole visited a toy fair in Copenhagen, Denmark. It was there that he came across an injection-molding machine used to mold plastic into shapes. The machine was very expensive—30,000 Danish kroner—which was how much **profit** LEGO had made in the last two

> **Profit:** A financial gain or amount of money a company or person has after all expenses have been paid. Sales minus costs equals profit.

years put together. Despite the high cost, Ole thought it was a good **investment** because

> **Investment:** Paying for something or putting money into something that you think will lead to profits in the future.

LEGO could make toys out of plastic, which would not absorb germs like wood and also be easier to clean. It was the solution he had been looking for.

When Ole bought the injection-molding machine, he also received samples of plastic self-locking building bricks that were made by the

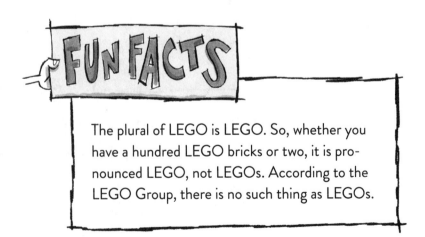

**FUN FACTS**

The plural of LEGO is LEGO. So, whether you have a hundred LEGO bricks or two, it is pronounced LEGO, not LEGOs. According to the LEGO Group, there is no such thing as LEGOs.

same type of machine. These bricks had been invented by a child psychologist named Hilary Fisher Page and sold by his company, Kiddicraft. The self-locking building bricks looked very similar to what LEGO bricks look like today, with a few

exceptions. The most obvious difference was the inside, which was a hollow square.

# 4

# A Snappy Idea

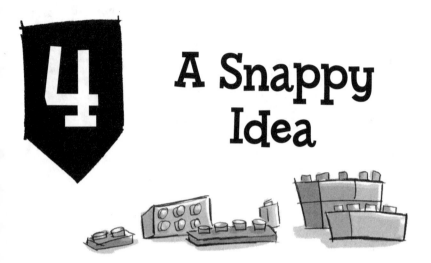

**A**s soon as the new injection-molding machine arrived, LEGO began producing little plastic animals and rattles. But Ole was fascinated with the plastic brick samples he had been given. He decided to launch a similar product. Ole and Godtfred worked together and redesigned the Kiddicraft brick. They

"Our idea has been to create a toy that prepares the child for life."
—Godtfred Christiansen

flattened the top studs, straightened out the edges, and changed the size by 0.1 millimeter. Ole called the new toy Automatic Binding Bricks.

LEGO launched Automatic Binding Bricks

 in 1949. They were made of cellulose acetate, a type of plastic, and came in four bright colors—white, red, yellow, and green. But much to Ole's dismay, Automatic Binding Bricks did not sell well. Come summertime, retailers had returned most of the sets unsold and the company became inundated with inventory.

This frustrated Godtfred. He believed that Automatic Binding Bricks were a good product and could be sold all year long, not just during the holiday season. In addition, Godtfred and his wife, Edith, had three young children at

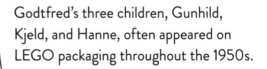

Godtfred's three children, Gunhild, Kjeld, and Hanne, often appeared on LEGO packaging throughout the 1950s.

home (Gunhild, born 1946; Kjeld, born 1947; and Hanne, born 1949), and he couldn't risk LEGO being in financial trouble. So Godtfred packed up his car with all the unsold LEGO sets and traveled around the country selling them door to door. He successfully unloaded much of the inventory and returned just in time to celebrate Ole's sixtieth birthday, where a famous photo was taken of Ole, Godtfred, and Godtfred's young son, Kjeld. (Remember Kjeld's name for later on!)

## A NEW MASTER BUILDER

Ole suffered a stroke shortly after his sixtieth birthday. With Ole's health declining, Godtfred took on a bigger leadership role at LEGO and

became junior managing director. Ole's other three sons, Johannes, Karl, and Gerhardt, also joined the company and were put in charge of different departments.

The four Christiansen brothers understood

**Brand equity:** Value that comes from the consumer's perception of a product with a particular name. Products with high brand equity have very loyal customers. Companies create brand equity by making their products or services memorable, easily recognizable, and superior in quality and reliability.

that there was **brand equity**, or value, in the name LEGO, so they decided to rename Automatic Binding Bricks and call them simply LEGO Bricks. They also molded the name LEGO into each of the bricks' studs. These changes helped improve sales a little, but LEGO Bricks still only accounted for 5 percent of the company's sales throughout the early 1950s.

## CREATING A SYSTEM

In 1954, Godtfred took a ferry ride across the North Sea to attend the London Toy Fair in England. It was there that he met a toy buyer

FUN FACTS

LEGO bricks made in 1955 still fit with LEGO bricks made today.

who worked for Magasin du Nord, the largest department store in Copenhagen, Denmark. The toy buyer insisted that there was a problem with toys in the world. Toys, he explained, needed a "system," or in other words, a way to work together. This idea intrigued Godtfred. He thought long and hard about how LEGO could create a "system" for toys.

After Godtfred returned to Denmark, he had an idea. Godtfred decided that LEGO

Bricks were going to become the foundation for a new system of toys. And instead of producing pre-made toys, such as a yo-yos, dolls, or wooden vehicles, LEGO would develop a way for children to *build their own* toys using LEGO's bricks. The "system" part of the idea meant that going forward, every individual LEGO brick would *always* fit together with every other LEGO brick, no matter what shape or size it was, or when or where it was made. The "system" also meant that LEGO would

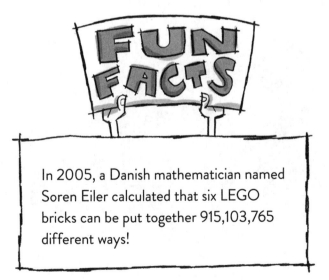

In 2005, a Danish mathematician named Soren Eiler calculated that six LEGO bricks can be put together 915,103,765 different ways!

provide instruction behind building a particular design but also give children the freedom to build whatever they wanted with the bricks. And the more bricks a child owned, the more possibilities he or she could create. The idea was revolutionary!

## LAYING THE FIRST BRICKS

In 1955, LEGO launched the LEGO System of Play. Each box contained an assortment

of LEGO bricks and a town plan. Children could follow the instructions for the town plan or build creations from their own imagination.

The LEGO System of Play became a huge hit in Denmark and Germany. But it wasn't all good news. Godtfred was now struggling with another problem. Although the LEGO bricks were fun to play with, children complained they did not stick together well. Remember that the insides were hollow, which made them easily stackable, but those stacks were fragile

and easily fell apart. Projects toppled over before they were finished, and kids couldn't move them from place to place without them collapsing into a pile of colorful bricks.

## A CLUTCH SOLUTION

Godtfred listened to this customer feedback and understood that he needed to find a way to make the bricks stick together. After many failed designs, he had an idea. Godtfred created a series of tubes inside the bricks that attached to the studs on top. The space between the hollow tubes and side walls was just a bit smaller than the studs themselves, so *friction*

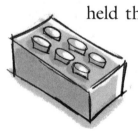

held the bricks together. Not only that, the interlocking bricks literally snapped together with a satisfying *click!* On January 28, 1958, Godtfred **patented** his stud and tube design in Denmark. Over time, he patented the design in thirty-two other countries, too. Each patent lasted for twenty years, which meant that no person or company could copy his design or create something similar to the LEGO Brick with its stud and tube design for twenty years.

Thanks to the power of friction, or what

## FUN FACTS

In 1981, the LEGO Group purchased the rights to the Kiddicraft brick from the company that invented the original plastic building brick.

Godtfred called "clutch power," children now could connect LEGO bricks together and know that their creations would not fall apart. Plus, children were no longer confined to building just towers and straight-edged buildings. Clutch power gave kids the ability to build in ways they never had before—from the bottom up, from the top down, sideways, backwards, or in separate sections. The invention of clutch power was a major turning point in the history of LEGO's success.

# Follow the Plastic Brick Road

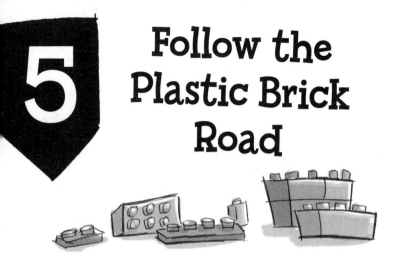

In 1957, LEGO celebrated its Jubilee, or twenty-fifth year. It was a happy time at the company, and despite his poor health, Ole was there to celebrate. That same year, Godtfred was promoted to managing director of LEGO.

Then, on March 11, 1958, Ole suffered

"You can go on and on, building and building. You never get tired of LEGO."
—An early LEGO advertising campaign

a heart attack and died at the age of sixty-six. Ole never got to see how LEGO would go on to change the world of toys forever. He also never got to see how much LEGO would better the lives of children around the globe and inspire future architects, engineers, and inventors. But Ole probably knew that his lessons of hard work, perseverance, and ingenuity would remain at the heart and soul of the company he left behind.

## THE THIRD FIRE

After Ole's death, Godtfred became the new director of LEGO. Business ran smoothly until two years later. On February 4, 1960, lightning struck another factory—the one where all the wooden toys were produced. By the time the massive fire was contained, it had destroyed everything.

The next day Godtfred made a hard decision. With the entire wooden toy inventory destroyed and another factory burnt beyond repair, he decided that LEGO would stop making wooden toys altogether. Godtfred believed that the future of LEGO lay in its little plastic bricks.

## LEGO REINVENTS THE WHEEL

Godtfred formed a **research and development** team called LEGO Futura, which was a small

**Research and development:** Often called R&D, this is an important part of any company. R&D refers to the work that goes toward the innovation, introduction, and improvement of new products. R&D teams dream up new ideas, test them with customers, and make suggestions for the next products to launch.

group of engineers and visionaries. Their job was to dream up, test, and launch new LEGO ideas.

Many new ideas evolved from LEGO Futura, such as hinge bricks, smooth tile pieces, arches, and a fence. But perhaps the most important invention of the decade was the LEGO wheel in 1961. Prior to creating a rubber wheel, children had used square bricks for tires, which did not roll. A real rubber wheel meant that

cars, airplanes, and train sets could move along the ground like the real thing. LEGO's rubber wheels were an instant success and soon included in every vehicle set.

LEGO Futura also created the idea for Duplo. These were oversize bricks designed for younger children with smaller hands. Exactly twice as big as the traditional LEGO brick, Duplo bricks were proportionally scaled so that they still fit within the LEGO system. Duplo became the perfect solution for preschoolers.

As the company expanded beyond Denmark, LEGO Futura developed wordless instructions. These were instruction booklets

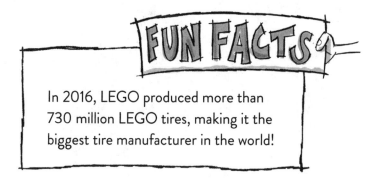

FUN FACTS

In 2016, LEGO produced more than 730 million LEGO tires, making it the biggest tire manufacturer in the world!

that included pictures and numbers *only*, making it easy for children of most ages to follow along, regardless of the language they spoke. In addition, wordless instructions put an emphasis on mathematical skills such as counting and measuring, which pleased parents and teachers alike.

LEGO Futura's new ideas proved that Ole's commitment to high quality and Godtfred's system of play could be expanded upon. These new products reached children of all ages and

made playing with LEGO more fun, regardless of the child's race, gender, religion, or nationality.

## LEGO TAKES OFF

Demand for LEGO continued to grow far beyond Denmark. That meant Godtfred was stuck with yet another challenge. He had to figure out a faster way to transport his products around the globe.

Today, Billund Airport is the second largest international airport in Denmark and has more than three million passengers each year.

In 1961, Godtfred bought a small plane and a field near the factories in Billund. The only problem was that since the field was not a real airport, it didn't have lights or electricity. That meant the pilots couldn't see where to land when it got too dark! Godtfred thought about this problem and came up with an idea.

He asked his employees to drive their cars over to the field and shine their headlights on the runway when a plane was due to land in the dark.

This, of course, was only a temporary solution. Before long, LEGO was sold in the United States, Canada, Japan, China, Australia, Latin America, and the Middle East. Godtfred needed to build a real airport, and in 1964, Billund Airport officially opened. Shipments of LEGO sets could now be flown to the rest of the world quickly and easily.

## LEGOLAND

By 1966, LEGO was sold in forty-two countries and the world was suddenly fascinated by everything LEGO. Each year more than 20,000 visitors arrived in Billund, Denmark, wanting a tour of the LEGO factory. Godtfred grew tired of these distractions and thought that if he built a small three-acre park nearby with some LEGO models, tourists would be satisfied. He would call it LEGOLAND.

On June 7, 1968, LEGOLAND opened

its doors. However, Godtfred's quaint LEGO park idea turned out to be far bigger and grander than he had  originally planned. Built on fourteen acres, it included hundreds of buildings and models of famous cities, all built from twenty million LEGO bricks. In addition, there were LEGO-themed rides and a LEGO train that encircled the park. With 3,000 visitors on its first day and 625,000 visitors the first year, LEGOLAND exceeded everyone's expectations.

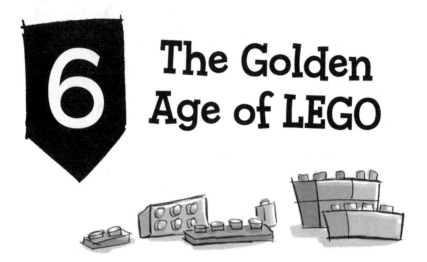

# 6 The Golden Age of LEGO

**S**ales at LEGO continued to grow throughout the 1970s under Godtfred's guidance. But as time went on, Godtfred started passing more leadership roles to his son and Ole's grandson, Kjeld (pronounced "Kell") Kirk Kristiansen.

"Children are our role models."
—LEGO slogan

(Kjeld's last name is spelled differently because of a typo on his birth certificate.)

In 1979, Kjeld was appointed CEO and president of the LEGO Group. Under Kjeld's leadership, the company entered the "Golden Age of LEGO"—when **revenues** grew from $142 million in 1978 to more than $1.2 billion in 1993. During that time, LEGO based everything it did on the three founding principles that Ole and Godtfred had set in place. One, LEGO was not a toy, but rather a "system of play." That meant *every single* LEGO piece worked together no matter when or where it was made. Two, every new LEGO set must be focused on *play,* which meant it gave children the chance to be creative and use their

> **Revenues:** Also called sales, revenues consist of all the money that is collected from selling a product or service.

imagination. And three, LEGO reinforced its high quality standards for all its toys. As Ole had famously stated, "Only the best is good enough."

## EXPANDING BEYOND THE BRICK

The Golden Age of LEGO was an exciting time, when many new ideas were introduced for children of all ages, with different interests and abilities. For example, LEGO created the "system within a system" and announced three different themes—Town, Castle, and Space—which became instant hits. They allowed children to build around a specific theme and then reuse the pieces to create something from their own imagination. The company launched LEGO Technic sets for older children who wanted a harder building challenge. The sets included beams, gears, axles, and pins. But perhaps the greatest invention of the 1970s was the minifigure.

## MINIFIGURES CONQUER THE WORLD

In 1974, LEGO created the "LEGO Family," which introduced a mother, father, grandmother, and children. The only problem was that these plastic people were proportionally too tall and towered over the houses and stores that children built from sets.

In 1975, LEGO launched its first "minifigure"—a more appropriate, proportionally sized person. However, these armless people lacked detail, facial expression, and movable limbs. The entire bottom half was just a solid piece of plastic.

Kjeld liked the concept of minifigures being included in LEGO sets. He believed that with a better design, they would enhance play and could even become collectibles.

After fifty different **prototypes**, LEGO released the new and improved minifigure in 1978. The first authentic minifigure was a policeman with two dots for eyes and a slight grin. His uniform consisted of a simple black torso with matching pants and a white hat. The first female minifigure arrived soon thereafter. She was a nurse with dark hair and the exact same

**Prototype:** A preliminary model of a product. Prototypes act as work-in-process products that allow designers and engineers to physically see what works and what doesn't. Some companies, such as Google, release prototypes of their products to their customers and use customer feedback to help make improvements and changes for the next version.

face as the policeman. In fact, all minifigures had the same simple eyes and smiling grin (no nose!) for eleven years.

Scaled appropriately, minifigures now stood exactly four centimeters—or four bricks tall—from head to toe. (Hats, hair pieces, and smaller "kid legs" changed the height.) Each minifigure was constructed with six main parts—head, torso, hips, legs, arms, and hands—and each part was designed to move in a very specific way. With these changes, minifigures had become an official part of the LEGO system.

FUN FACTS

In 2007, the LEGO Group made 10,000 special gold chrome C-3PO minifigures and randomly inserted them in Star Wars sets. Do you have one at home?

# MINIFIGURES GET REAL

In 1989, LEGO's pirate line launched, the first minifigures to have more realistic facial expressions. Pirate minifigures were also the first of their kind to include special accessories, in this case hooks for hands and pegs for legs.

More LEGO accessories were added over the years. They ranged from all types of hats and hairstyles to a wide variety of things to hold. And while many sets include a "good guy" and a "bad guy," you will never find a modern gun or weapon because that goes against LEGO's principles of wholesome play.

Instead, LEGO arms its minifigures with weapons that take some creativity to ignite, such as medieval swords, old-fashioned guns from the Wild West, or futuristic weapons such as Star Wars lightsabers.

Colors, too, started to change. The original minifigure was created yellow, a color chosen to represent equality among all people on earth and not intended to represent any one race. Over the years, the color has been altered only when the minifigure is supposed to portray a real person, such as a professional athlete, or a character from a movie like Harry Potter or Yoda.

Minifigures are a huge success. Since their conception, billions of minifigures have been produced. When the minifigure turned twenty-

five years old in 2003, LEGO announced that 3.7 billion minifigures had been produced. Some estimate that the total number of minifigures produced will soon reach eight billion—more than there are people in the world!

# 7 LEGO Falls Apart

In its first sixty years, the LEGO Group had grown from a small workshop in Denmark to an international billion-dollar business and one of the largest toy manufacturers in the world, with thousands of employees. In 1989, LEGO sets were sold in over 120 countries, and tens of millions of children played with

"Ouch!"
—Anyone who has stepped on a LEGO brick with bare feet

LEGO bricks every year. But then a series of challenges arose, and for the first time in decades, the LEGO Group started to struggle.

## WHAT WENT WRONG

LEGO's last patent expired in 1989. That meant other companies could produce products similar to LEGO's bricks. Before long, companies such as Mega Bloks, Best-Lock, and Tyco Toys had entered stores with their own version of interlocking brick sets.

The onset of new and often less expensive competition sent LEGO scrambling, and the company began to lose focus. Instead of staying dedicated to what it did best, LEGO started to chase the newest trend of the 1990s—video and computer games. They released LEGO

video games, computer-controlled robots, and pre-made toys that didn't require building. The company opened new LEGOLAND theme parks in England, California, and Germany, launched a clothing line, and even sold LEGO watches. Instead of staying true to its system of play, LEGO had gotten lost in trying to be something it was not.

Executives within the LEGO Group also made some drastic changes. They fired many of the key designers responsible for the growth of the 1970s and 1980s and hired young designers from top universities. However, these new designers did not understand the history of LEGO and what made it so special. And they did not keep costs in mind when developing new LEGO sets. Before long, thousands of elaborate and complicated pieces had been invented, many of which were expensive to make. In some cases, the unique pieces within a set cost more to produce than the entire set was sold for! As you can imagine, a company can't make a profit if its costs exceed its sales price. The LEGO Group started losing money—lots of money.

And then, sadly, Godtfred passed away at the age of seventy-five on July 13, 1995.

In 1998, LEGO posted a loss of 194 million kroner, or $27.7 million, the company's first loss since being founded in 1932. That meant LEGO had more costs (194 million kroner more) than sales that year. And sales continued to fall. In 2003, LEGO's sales dropped 1.4 billion kroner, or 25 percent, from its previous year. On top of that, tourism was way down at LEGOLAND. It seemed that children and families had fallen out of love with LEGO. Within ten years, LEGO had gone from an international leader in the toy industry to a company heading for **bankruptcy**. Many thought LEGO was doomed.

**Bankruptcy:** When a company (or person) does not have enough money to pay its debts.

# BUSINESS BASICS

What's the difference between sales and profits?

 **SALES**—Also called revenue. Sales consist of all the money that is collected from selling a product or service.

**COSTS**—Also called expenses or expenditures. Costs are the funds required to run a business or company. These include any direct costs incurred in the production of the goods sold, such as the price of materials used to make the product, the cost of labor and other salaries, and expenditures for rent and advertising.

 **BREAKEVEN**—The point reached when sales minus costs equals zero; in other words, the point at which total sales are equal to total costs.

**PROFIT**—The point at which sales minus costs equals a figure greater than zero.

Take, for example, a lemonade stand. Before you start selling lemonade, you'll need to buy cups ($3) and lemonade mix ($2). You borrow your mom's pitcher ($0). Your **costs** are $5. The price you decide to charge for each cup of lemonade is 50 cents.

If you sell ten cups of lemonade (ten x 50 cents), your **sales** will be $5. But that amount equals your **costs** (cups + lemonade mix = $5). At ten cups of lemonade, you **break even**. At eleven cups of lemonade sold, or $5.50, you now have made a **profit** of 50 cents. Keep selling to make more profit!

# 8 Rebuilding LEGO's Foundation

LEGO was in trouble and Kjeld knew it. He needed to do something drastic to turn the business around. In 2004, Kjeld appointed a man named Jorgen Vig Knudstorp as the CEO. This marked the first time someone outside of the Christiansen family would lead the LEGO Group.

"Children mean everything to us. Children and their development."
—Kjeld Kirk Kristiansen

With Jorgen in charge, several changes occurred. Jorgen divested, or sold off, different parts of the company that were either unpopular or didn't correspond with LEGO's system of play. The LEGO Group sold its computer and video game divisions, as well as its clothing and watch businesses. Jorgen also sold LEGOLAND, which was expensive to operate and losing money. Moving forward, Jorgen insisted that every single product LEGO made

must fall within its system of play and be compatible with one another, just like Ole and Godtfred had intended from the beginning.

Next, Jorgen focused on cutting costs. He eliminated the unique pieces that were expensive to produce. He also reduced the overall number of bricks the company made by half. That meant LEGO designers could create new sets using a family of 6,000 elements rather than 12,000. These changes quickly helped improve the company's profitability.

# FUN FACTS

It would take more than forty billion bricks to build a LEGO tower to the moon.

# RECONNECTING WITH FANS

Jorgen recognized another big problem—the company had lost touch with its core fans. By hiring designers in the 1990s who didn't have a personal allegiance to LEGO, much of the magic and history behind the brand had disappeared.

Jorgen believed that if he employed LEGO

fans to be the designers of new products, the company would produce sets that other fans wanted *and* bring back excitement to the brand. The LEGO Group held its first designer recruitment workshop and hired eleven individuals who were devoted to LEGO. These self-proclaimed AFOLs (Adult Fans of LEGO) grew up playing with LEGO sets, and they understood the history behind LEGO and what made the system of play work. But perhaps most important, these AFOL designers were superior builders with lots of new, creative ideas.

Within a few short years, Jorgen's changes had reconnected LEGO to its roots. The company was again focused on its successful system of play. New theme sets such as Star Wars, Harry Potter, Ninjago, and LEGO Friends launched to the delight of fans around the world. The LEGO Group also formed a partnership with  Disney to create Disney-themed LEGO sets ranging from Disney princesses to the Disney castle, and the company had positive sales growth once again.

## FUN FACTS

The figures that come in LEGO Friends sets are called mini-dolls and not considered minifigures because they have more realistic proportions.

# 9 Everything Is Awesome

From 2004 to 2014, sales quadrupled under Jorgen's leadership. The LEGO Group had become one of the biggest toy companies in the world, and fans had fallen back in love with the brand and created a LEGO world all their own. With conventions, clubs, and competitions, there was no limit to what

"It's not a toy. It's a highly sophisticated interlocking brick system." —*The LEGO Movie*

fans would build or create together. Across the globe, people held LEGO boat races, LEGO derby car races, and building competitions—sometimes blindfolded! Schools created LEGO robotics clubs, libraries sponsored LEGO building activities, and adults (AFOLs) created their own conventions, such as BrickWorld and BrickFest.

People were inspired to build anything and everything out of LEGO bricks. One man in Romania built the first working LEGO car. One of Google's founders, Larry Page, built a working ink printer out of LEGO bricks

when he was in college. And a man in England built a real house using three million LEGO bricks. It came with LEGO utensils, a working LEGO toilet, and even a (very uncomfortable) LEGO bed.

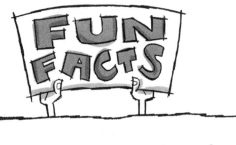

The biggest LEGO model ever built was a Star Wars spaceship that took 17,000 hours to create. It measured forty-four feet wingtip to wingtip and forty-five feet from bow to stern.

# MAKING A MOVIE

Then, in 2014, the LEGO Group did something that changed the company forever. It released its first feature-length film—*The LEGO Movie*. Inspired by stop-motion brick films, which had become popular on YouTube, *The LEGO Movie* took more than eight years to make and combined animation with real LEGO pieces. In fact, *everything* in the movie was either a real LEGO piece or animated to look exactly like one. A total of 3,863,484 LEGO pieces were used, for everything from soap bars to lasers to a molten lava floor.

*The LEGO Movie* introduced a minifigure named Emmet who mistakenly became the storyline's chosen one, also known  as "the Special." The film featured well-known charac- ters such as Batman and Dumbledore, and even President Abraham Lincoln—making him the first ever minifigure president. *The LEGO Movie* brought humor and joy to fans young and old, received rave reviews

The first LEGO store opened in 1992 at the Mall of America in Bloomington, Minnesota. Originally called the LEGO Imagination Center, it included LEGO sculptures, an open play area where children could build with bins of LEGO bricks, and sets for sale.

from movie critics, and launched a new level of LEGO excitement across the globe. The movie also helped sales. Following its release, the LEGO Group experienced a 15 percent sales increase. And in 2015, LEGO passed Mattel to become the number one toy company in the entire world.

# Beyond the Brick

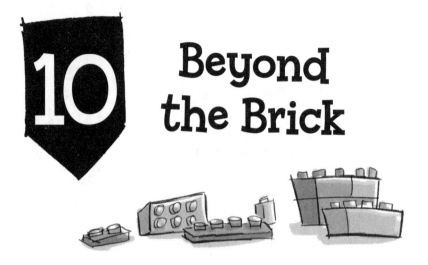

Over time, LEGO has proven to be more than a toy. It is also a tool that helps people invent, express themselves, solve problems, and communicate. Enter just about any elementary school classroom and you will find LEGO bricks. Teachers supply them not only as a fun activity, but also to spark imagination

"The possibilities for LEGO Architecture are almost limitless."
—Adam Reed Tucker, master builder and founder of LEGO Architecture

and teach students how to problem solve, count, and work together. Artists use them to create, sculpt, and express themselves. Doctors have found LEGO bricks help autistic children communicate with others. Even NASA scientists and engineers build spaceships and space equipment out of LEGO pieces as part of the design process. And sometimes a LEGO creation can turn into a business of its own . . .

# BRICK ENTREPRENEUR

For more than a decade, an architect named Adam Reed Tucker designed luxury homes and impressive buildings. During that time, he realized that the world of architecture was turning digital. Physical models and hand drawings were being replaced with computer models and digital drawings.

In 2006, Adam longed to build *real* models

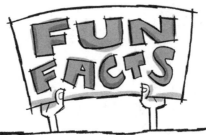

Adam Reed Tucker created giant LEGO replicas of a dozen landmarks, including a sixty-foot Golden Gate Bridge, the International Space Station, and the Roman Colosseum. They were featured in a special exhibit at the Museum of Science & Industry in Chicago.

of buildings. He was particularly inspired by prominent architectural structures in big cities. But before he began, Adam needed a medium, a material with which to work. He wanted it to be easy to use, strong, durable, and not require any cutting, painting, or gluing. And then it dawned on him—LEGO bricks!

At the time, it was unheard of to build architectural models from LEGO bricks. They were still primarily considered a child's toy. But Adam had other ideas. Inspired by the art of Leonardo da Vinci, the imagination of Walt Disney, and the creativity of Willy Wonka, he rushed out to his local Toys "R" Us store and purchased every single LEGO set in the store, ultimately filling up eleven shopping carts. Adam worked day and night to create his first architectural structure—an enormous model

of Chicago's Sears Tower (now called the Willis Tower) made entirely from LEGO bricks.

He displayed his new piece at BrickFest, where he met an executive from the LEGO Group named Paal Smith-Meyer. Paal was impressed. Together, they had an idea. If Adam could shrink the models down to a size that would fit into a small box, the LEGO Group might be able to sell them.

Adam went home and got to work. He labored for weeks, creating several new, small models, including ones of the Empire State Building, Seattle's Space Needle, and Chicago's John Hancock Center. The LEGO Group was thrilled with the mini-models, and before long they launched a new product line called LEGO Architecture.

The mini-replicas of historical buildings

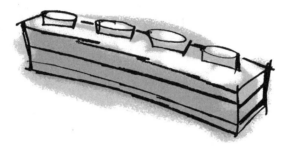

flew off the shelves. Sales of LEGO Architecture increased 900 percent from its first year to its second year. The reason was twofold. One, LEGO Architecture attracted different customers. Most people who bought these unique sets were adults, intrigued by the creative new use for LEGO bricks. Two, LEGO Architecture opened new **distribution channels** for the company. LEGO Architecture was

**Distribution channels:** A business that helps sell a company's products or services to the end consumer. Distribution channels can include retail stores, wholesalers, catalogues, and the Internet.

sold in places LEGO sets had never been sold before, such as souvenir shops, museums, and big book stores like Barnes & Noble.

Today, architectural fans can build just about anything, from Buckingham Palace in London, England, and the Eiffel Tower in Paris, France, to the White House in Washington, DC. "There are so many landmark structures, both ancient and modern, throughout our built environment," Adam explained. "Architecture transcends race, religion, age—it really knows no boundaries. So the possibilities for LEGO Architecture are almost limitless."

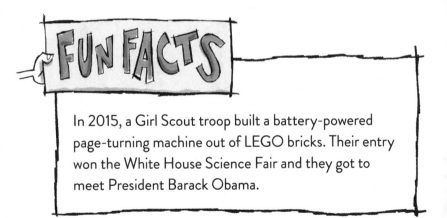

In 2015, a Girl Scout troop built a battery-powered page-turning machine out of LEGO bricks. Their entry won the White House Science Fair and they got to meet President Barack Obama.

# 11 Building a Better World

LEGO is the story of a simple toy that became so much more. Ole built his first wooden toy in 1932. Over time, the LEGO Group expanded into plastic, invented stud and tube "clutch power," launched mini-figures, and produced an award-winning film created entirely from its system of play. But

"We want to build a future where learning through play empowers children to become creative, engaged, lifelong learners."
—The LEGO Foundation

LEGO is more than a worldwide phenomenon. It's a tool that children, adults, teachers, scientists, artists, doctors, and architects use every day, because the possibilities for learning with LEGO are endless. And that's where the LEGO **Foundation** comes in.

> **Foundation:** A charitable organization that typically donates funds and resources to support a philanthropic mission or other charitable organization.

## THE LEGO FOUNDATION

The LEGO Foundation originally launched in 1986 with the belief that all children should have the right to play. At first, the LEGO Foundation focused on donating products to those less fortunate. Today, the LEGO Foundation has stretched its goals to reach as many children as possible around the globe and make their lives better through play. Its mission is to "build a future where learning through play empowers children to become creative, engaged, life-long learners." The LEGO Foundation has three programs in place: One program educates parents and teachers on the benefits of play in early childhood. A second program makes the connection between play

You could create the next LEGO set. Upload your creation on LEGO's website, and if you receive 10,000 votes of support, a LEGO committee will review your design. Each year, the committee chooses one new set to be launched to the world. And the creator receives a portion of the profits! Good luck!

and high-quality education. The third program focuses on creating communities around the world that are based on learning through play. In each instance, the LEGO Foundation donates time, money, and LEGO products, and shares research studies that link play with creative, engaging, and lifelong learning skills.

## LEGO TODAY

LEGO is one of the greatest entrepreneurial success stories of all time. And one that was built on the principles of quality, hard work, and a system of play.

It all began with a dedicated carpenter named Ole Kirk Christiansen who persevered through multiple setbacks and followed his passion to make high-quality toys for children.

His commitment and loyalty to his family, employees, and customers set the values and principles for a company that would go on to change the world for the better.

Over time, Ole and his son Godtfred created a system of play and a revolutionary interlocking brick design that gave the company the power to grow internationally. Under the guidance of Ole's grandchild Kjeld, LEGO introduced minifigures and entered a period of growth known as the Golden Age of LEGO. However, when executives tried to shift the

The LEGO Group continues to search for ways to replace the oil-based material used to make its bricks with a more environmentally friendly solution.

company away from its core system of play, LEGO stumbled and almost went bankrupt.

In 2004, the LEGO Group's first non–family member led the company to a new era of growth by refocusing its product line, launching *The LEGO Movie*, and expanding its mission to help others learn through play. Since then, a new CEO has taken over, and the company has released four more hit films: *The LEGO Batman Movie, The LEGO Ninjago Movie, The LEGO Movie 2: The Second Part,* and *The Billion Brick Race,* to fans' delight.

Today, the LEGO Group is the biggest toy company in the world. Every second, seven new LEGO sets are sold. Every minute, LEGO factories produce 36,000 bricks. And every year, children and adults play with LEGO's minifigures, theme sets, and pieces for five billion hours. That's a lot of play. And that's a lot of LEGO!

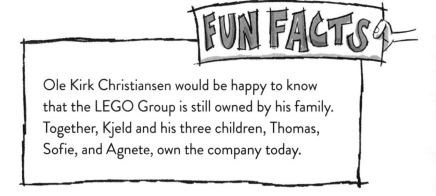

Ole Kirk Christiansen would be happy to know that the LEGO Group is still owned by his family. Together, Kjeld and his three children, Thomas, Sofie, and Agnete, own the company today.

Seeing the joy in children as they play with LEGO bricks is truly special, but what gives real meaning to our work is knowing that we are nurturing the skills to help the next generation shape the world."
—Niels B. Christiansen, CEO, the LEGO Group

# TIMELINE OF LEGO

**1891** • Ole Kirk Christiansen is born in Denmark on April 7.

**1905** • Ole starts his training as a carpenter.

**1916** • Ole buys the Billund Carpentry Shop and Lumberyard in Denmark.

**1924** • The first fire burns down Ole's factory and house.

**1930** • The Great Depression hits and sales decline. Ole is forced to lay off all his employees.

**1932** • Ole's wife, Kirstine, dies. Ole is raising his four sons alone and has an idea to build wooden toys.

**1934** • Ole names his toy company LEGO. The word combines the two words in the Danish term *leg godt*—which means "play well."

**1942** • On March 20, a second fire burns down the LEGO factory.

**1947** • Ole purchases a plastic molding machine and LEGO begins to make and sell plastic toys and rattles.

**1949** • LEGO launches "Automatic Binding Bricks."

**1951** • Ole suffers a stroke. Godtfred Christiansen takes on more leadership roles at LEGO.

**1953** • The name LEGO is first molded into every LEGO brick.

**1954** • Godtfred decides that LEGO bricks should be part of a universal system of play.

**1958** • Ole dies of a heart attack on March 11. Godtfred becomes the new director of LEGO and redesigns the LEGO brick to include a "stud and tube" shape, which helps the bricks stick together with clutch power.

**1960** • A third fire burns down the factory where LEGO's wooden toys are produced. Godtfred decides to discontinue all wooden toys.

**1961** • The LEGO wheel is invented. LEGO starts selling in the United States and Canada.

**1964** • Billund Airport officially opens. Wordless building instructions are included in LEGO sets.

**1967** • LEGO Duplo is launched.

**1968** • The first LEGOLAND opens in Billund, Denmark, on June 7.

**1975** • The first minifigures are released, but they have no face, arms, or movable legs.

**1978–93** • The Golden Age of LEGO. Revenues grow from $142 million in 1978 to $1.2 billion in 1993.

**1978** • The updated minifigures launch with smiley expressions and movable limbs.

**1979** • Kjeld Kirk Kristiansen takes over as CEO of the LEGO Group.

**1995** • Godtfred dies on July 13.

**1998** • LEGO loses focus on its system of play and posts its first loss ever.

**2003** • LEGO loses over 1.4 billion kroner in one year, the company's worst year ever. The LEGO Group is on the verge of bankruptcy.

**2004** • Jorgen Vig Knudstorp becomes CEO of the LEGO Group.

**2005** • Jorgen sells off LEGOLAND theme parks, video games, clothing, and watches. He refocuses LEGO back to its traditional system of play.

**2009** • The LEGO Group partners with Disney.

**2012** • LEGO Friends launches.

**2014** • *The LEGO Movie* premieres.

**2015** • The LEGO Group becomes the biggest toy company in the world.

**2017** • The LEGO Group hits 35 billion kroner ($5.8 billion) in sales and 10.4 billion kroner ($1.7 billion) in profits. LEGO toys are sold in more than 140 countries, and the company employs 17,500 people from seventy different nationalities.

# How LEGO Bricks Are Made

The story of LEGO is, in fact, impressive. And, what's equally impressive is how one company makes all those unique plastic pieces that fit perfectly with one another. Here is how LEGO bricks are made . . .

It all starts with plastic granules composed of acrylonitrile butadiene styrene, or ABS. Trucks filled with different-colored granules arrive at the LEGO factory, where giant hoses vacuum them up and store them in enormous silos.

FUN FACTS

One machine can spit out 15,000 minifigure heads an hour.

**MOLDING:** As needed, the granules travel through tubes or pipes to the injection molding machines. There, the granules are heated up to 450°F (232°C), which turns them into a melted goopy substance. The hot goop is fed into metal molds, kind of the way you pour water into an ice cube tray to make ice. Next, the machine applies between 25 and 150 tons of pressure. This cools the newly formed LEGO pieces. Once cooled, they are ejected from the mold, topple onto a conveyor belt, and fall into the correct bin. The entire process of HEAT—MOLD—COOL—EJECT takes less than ten seconds!

**PRINTING:** When the bin is filled with new LEGO elements, a robot transports it into the assembly hall. Here, machines assemble complex pieces such as minifigure legs and hips, which need to be snapped

together. This is also where printing takes place and minifigures receive their unique facial expression and clothing design.

**PACKAGING:** The final step is packaging, where all the correct pieces get placed into small plastic bags and dropped into the appropriate set. To make this happen, automated bins open and close, dropping the exact quantity and type of brick into each bag. Packing operators fold the box, add instructions, and make sure the right bags are placed into the box. Finally, the boxes are sealed and shipped around the world to toy stores, LEGO stores, and children like you!

# Source Notes

### Chapter 1—Ole Kirk Christiansen

2    *"Life is a gift"*: Hoque, "How LEGO Survived Against All Odds."

7    *gardening and beekeeping:* "1916–1929 Ole Kirk Kristiansen Settles in Billund," www.lego.com/en-us/legohistory/ole-settles-in-billund, accessed January 29, 2018.

### Chapter 2—Construction Begins

12    *"Not until the day":* Lipkowitz, *The LEGO Book,* p. 10.

17    *one of seven categories:* Keller, *Strategic Brand Management,* p. 183.

### Chapter 3—Brick by Brick

23    *"I look to the future with hope":* "1929–1932 Dealing with the Crisis," www.lego.com/en-us/legohistory/dealing-with-the-crisis, accessed January 29, 2018.

24    *sales doubled:* "The Beginning of the LEGO Group," www.lego.com/en-us/legohistory/the-beginning-of-the-lego-group, accessed January 29, 2018.

### Chapter 4—A Snappy Idea

32    *"Our idea has been to create a toy"*: Robertson, *Brick by Brick*, p. 23.

     *They flattened the top studs:* Ibid, p. 19.

34    *could be sold all year long:* "The LEGO Story." www.you tube.com/watch?v=NdDU_BBJW9Y&t=12s, accessed January 29, 2018.

37    *They also molded the name LEGO:* Hugo, *Absolutely Everything You Need to Know*, p. 10.

39    *In 2005, a Danish mathematician:* "The LEGO System," www.brickfetish.com/timeline/1958.html, accessed January 29, 2018.

### Chapter 5—Follow the Plastic Brick Road

45    *"You can go on and on":* Robertson, *Brick by Brick*, p. 22.

49    *more than 730 million LEGO tires:* Hugo, *Absolutely Everything You Need to Know*, p. 14.

53    *drive their cars over to the field:* Hagar, *Awesome Minds*, p. 44.

## Chapter 6—The Golden Age of LEGO

56 *"Children are our role models"*: Robertson, *Brick by Brick*, p. 28.

57 *"Golden Age of LEGO"—when revenues grew:* Robertson, "Building Success."

65 *3.7 billion minifigures had been produced:* "LEGO Minifigure Turns 25," www.lego.com/en-us/aboutus/news-room/2003/october/lego-minifigure-turns-25, accessed January 25, 2018.

## Chapter 9—Everything Is Awesome

83 *a total of 3,863,484 LEGO pieces were used:* Tsai, "Here's How the Animators Made *The LEGO Movie*."

## Chapter 10—Beyond the Brick

86 *"The possibilities for LEGO Architecture"*: Robertson, *Brick by Brick*, p. 211.

94 *"There are so many landmark structures"*: Ibid.

*In 2015, a Girl Scout troop built:* Friedman, "Girl Scouts Impress Obama."

# Bibliography

Anstruther, Jen, Jonathan Green, Kate Lloyd, and Simon Guerrier. *I Love That Minifigure.* New York: DK Publishing, 2015.

Farshtey, Gregory, and Daniel Lipkowitz. *LEGO Minifigure Year by Year: A Visual History.* New York: DK Publishing, 2013.

Friedman, Dan. "Girl Scouts Impress Obama with LEGO Device That Turns Pages." *Daily News,* March 23, 2015.

Hagar, Erin. *Awesome Minds: The Inventors of LEGO Toys.* New York: Duo Press, 2016.

Hoque, Faisal. "How LEGO Survived Against All Odds—and You Can, Too." FastCompany.com, March 10, 2014. www.fastcompany.com/3027147/how-lego-survived-against-all-odds-and-you-can-too.

Hugo, Simon. *Absolutely Everything You Need to Know.* New York: DK Publishing, 2017.

Keller, Kevin Lane. *Strategic Brand Management.* Upper Saddle River, NJ: Pearson Education, 2003.

Lipkowitz, Daniel. *The LEGO Book.* New York: DK Publishing Special Markets, 2009.

Robertson, David C. *Brick by Brick*. New York: Crown Publishing, 2013.

———. "Building Success: How Thinking 'Inside the Brick' Saved LEGO." *Wired*, October 9, 2013. www.wired.co.uk /article/building-success.

Tsai, Diane. "Here's How the Animators Made *The LEGO Movie*." *Time*, February 20, 2014. entertainment.time .com/2014/02/20/how-the-lego-movie-was-made -animation-video.

# Web Sources

LEGO.com

LEGOFoundation.com

History of LEGO: Wikipedia.org/wiki/History_of_LEGO

How LEGO Bricks Work: entertainment.howstuffworks.com /LEGO.htm

The LEGO Story: www.youtube.com/watch?v=NdDU _BBJW9Y

**Lowey Bundy Sichol** is the author and creator of **From an IDEA to . . .** , the world's first business biography series for kids. She is also the founder of Case Marketing, a specialized writing firm that composes case studies for business schools. Her case studies have been read by business school students all over the world. Lowey received an MBA from the Tuck School of Business at Dartmouth and a BA from Hamilton College. She lives in Illinois with her husband, Adam, three children, and two big dogs whose tails can take down just about any LEGO structure. Look for her online at LoweyBundySichol.com.

**FUN FACTS**

If Lowey was a minifigure, she'd have a pony-tail, a big smile, a softball mitt in one hand, and a copy of *From an Idea to LEGO* in the other.

**FUN FACTS**

When Lowey's kids were younger, they created some imaginative LEGO sets of their own, including a Western saloon, a hair salon, and a bus made for 20 minifigures. Visit LoweyBundySichol.com for pictures of them.

**FUN FACTS**

Lowey lives not far from the founder of LEGO Architecture, Adam Reed Tucker. Even crazier, Lowey's husband's name is Adam, her brother's name is Reed, and her son's name is Tucker.

# FROM AN IDEA TO

# DISNEY

How Imagination Built
a World of Magic

by **LOWEY BUNDY SICHOL**

illustrated by **C. S. JENNINGS**

# FROM AN IDEA TO

# NIKE

How Marketing Made
Nike a Global Success

by **LOWEY BUNDY SICHOL**
illustrated by **C. S. JENNINGS**

# FROM AN IDEA TO GOOGLE

How Innovation at Google Changed the World

by LOWEY BUNDY SICHOL

illustrated by C. S. JENNINGS